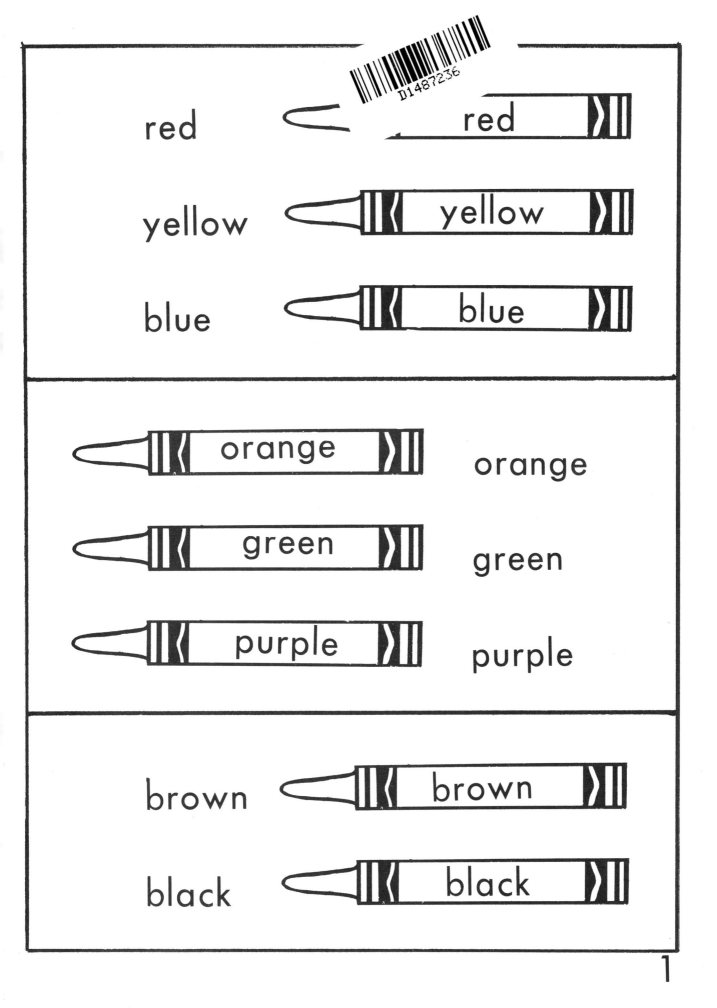

red red

yellow yellow

blue blue

orange orange

green green

purple purple

brown brown

black black

ship

shop

shell

shelf

shack

shade

sheep

sheep   the
shelf   The
on   is

The   the
is   shell
on   shack

_____ _____ _____

The ship is blue.

The shelf is yellow.

The shack is brown.

The sheep is black.

The shell is red.

The shade is green.

  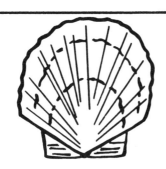

_____ _____ _____

trash

splash

fish

brush

leash

paintbrush   hairbrush

wishbone   scrub brush

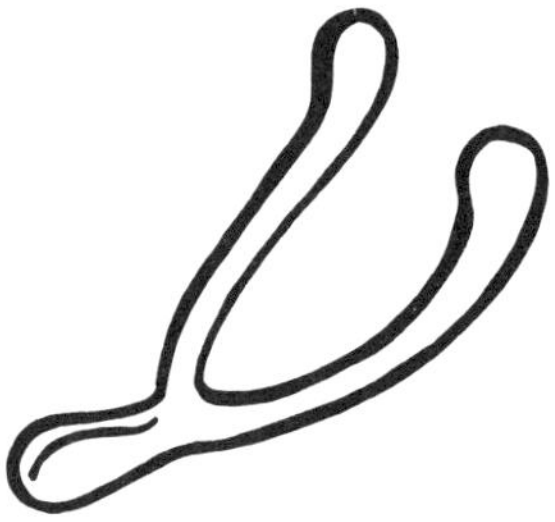

_____   _____

_____   _____

6

		trap trash
		leap leash
		fish fist
		shop stop

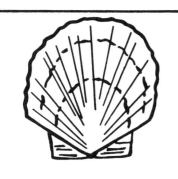

_____ _____ _____

The shack is purple.

The ship is blue.

The brush is red.

The shell is yellow.

The sheep is brown.

The fish is green.

_____ _____ _____

Now you can read the storybook *Fish Fun* listed on the back cover.

chair   chess

cheese   check

chill   sandwich

_____   _____

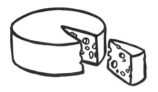

_____   _____

_____   _____

chop

chain

chick

chest

chums

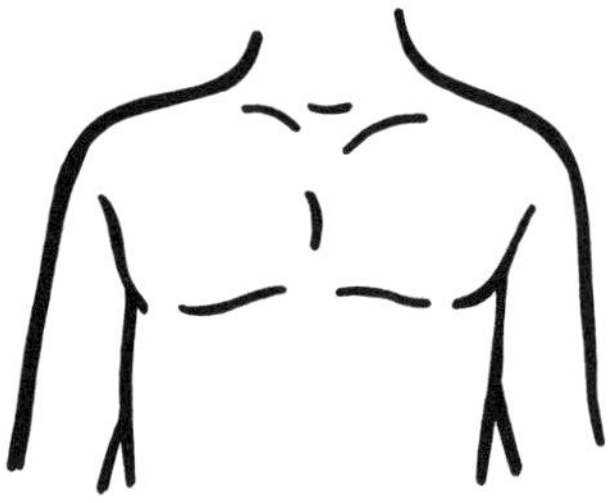

_____   _____

_____   _____

_____

fish   is
The   cheese
the   on

The   chick
is   the
on   sheep

_____	_____	_____

The cheese is yellow.

The leash is green.

The chair is red.

The chick is yellow.

The fish is brown.

The check is blue.

_____	_____	_____

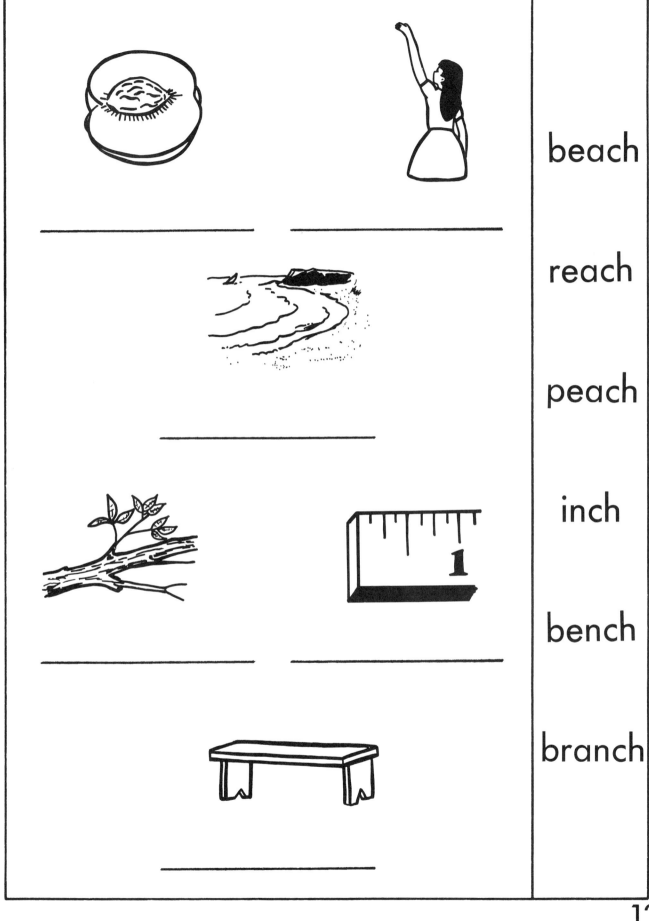

beach

reach

peach

inch

bench

branch

Five sheep are yellow.

Six sheep are brown.

14

witch　　　　　　　　match

hatch　　　　　　　　latch

kitchen

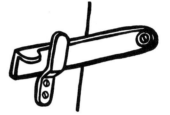

_____ _____ _____

The chick is yellow.

The match is red.

The kitchen is green.

The witch is black.

The bench is brown.

The peach is orange.

_____ _____ _____

match	the
is	chick
The	on

The	cheese
is	the
on	sheep

17

_____

_____

_____

The sheep is orange.

The chair is yellow.

The brush is brown.

The chick is blue.

The fish is red.

The cheese is purple.

_____

_____

_____

18

Now you can read the storybook *The Chicken Ranch* listed on the back cover.

king

sing

ring

wing

swing

string

sting

string street		 _____
swing sweep	 _____	 _____
branch brush	 _____	 _____
trash train	 _____	 _____

ink

wink

sink

mink

drink

pink

ink inch		
wink wing		
sink sing		
milk mink		

sank

bank

drink

bunk

trunk

skunk

_____

_____

_____

The sink is green.

The ink is black.

The trunk is brown.

The ring is yellow.

The bank is green.

The king is red.

_____

_____

_____

chipmunk   lipstick

lunch box   wish bone

_____   _____

_____   _____

skunk skate	 _____	 _____
track trunk	 _____	 _____
wing witch	 _____	 _____
bench beach	 _____	 _____

	Yes	No
Is the fish on the train?		
Is the chick on the chair?		
Is the skunk on the chair?		
Is the fish on the sink?		
Is the skunk on the train?		
Is the chick on the sink?		

The fish is green.
The skunk is black.
The train is orange.
The chick is brown.
The chair is blue.
The sink is yellow.

sing string ___	swing sweep ___
bunk bank ___	cheese chess ___
sheep ship ___	kitten kitchen ___
king kite ___	sandwich sunset ___

Now you can read the storybook *Ring the Bell* listed on the back cover.

kettle   paddle

rattle   saddle

bottle

_____   _____

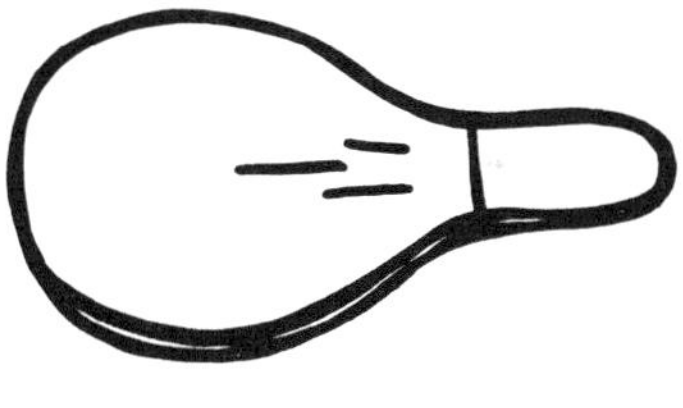

_____   _____

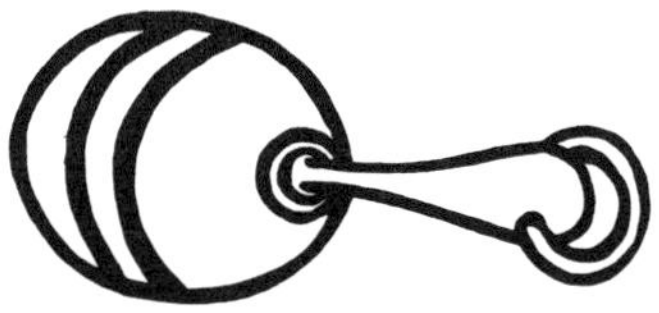

_____

_____

_____

The kettle is yellow.

The lipstick is yellow.

The chipmunk is brown.

The rattle is blue.

_____

_____

pineapple	apple
candle	needle

_____

_____

_____

_____

_____

_____

The candle is green.

The pineapple is yellow.

The apple is red.

The saddle is brown.

_____

_____

		can
		candle
_____	_____	
		sad
		saddle
_____	_____	
		rat
		rattle
_____	_____	
		pad
		paddle
_____	_____	

33

Six apples are red.

Five apples are yellow.

thimble   teeth

three   bath

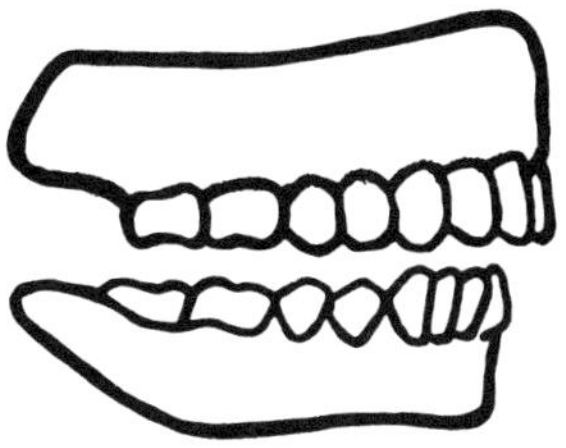

_____   _____

_____   _____

Three fish are green.

Three fish are yellow.

Three chicks are yellow.

Five chicks are brown.

wheel   whale

wheat   white

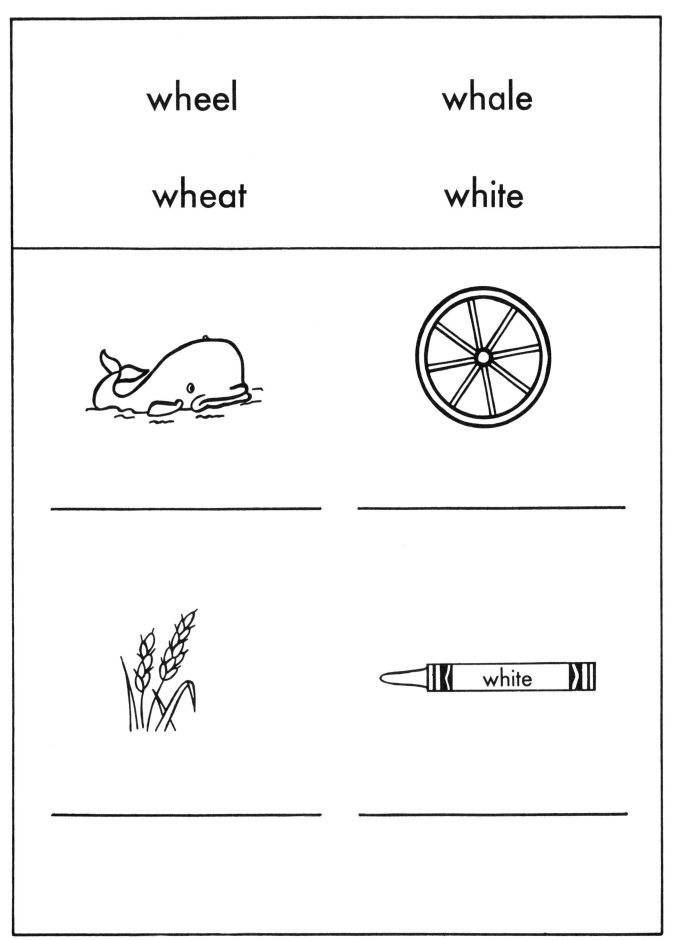

_____

_____

_____

_____

_____ _____ _____

The sink is green.

The king is red.

The three is orange.

The wheat is yellow.

The thimble is purple.

The whale is black.

_____ _____ _____

		tree
	3	three
_____	_____	

		wheat
		ship
_____	_____	

		white
white		witch
_____	_____	

		bank
		bath
_____	_____	

whale   wheel
The   the
is   on

the   on
The   is
three   teeth

Three candles are red.

Nine candles are green.

The peach is orange.

The teeth are yellow.

The wheel is brown.

The three is blue.

The sink is red.

The needle is purple.

  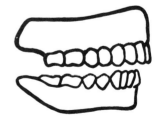

42

Now you can read the storybook *The White Hen* listed on the back cover.

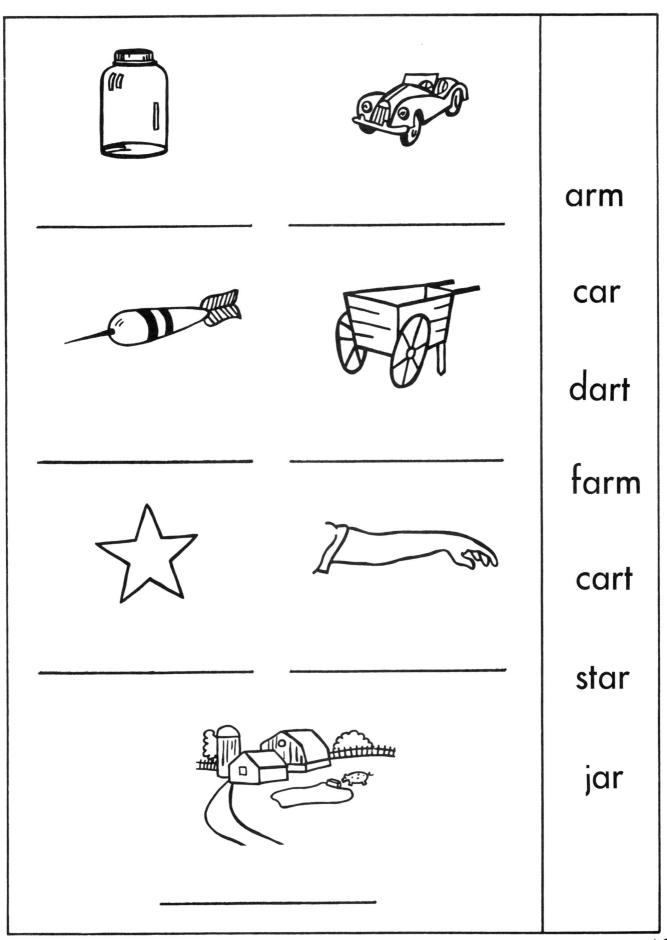

arm

car

dart

farm

cart

star

jar

43

_____

_____

_____

The cart is red.

The car is blue.

The arm is brown.

The star is yellow.

The jar is green.

The dart is orange.

_____

_____

_____

44

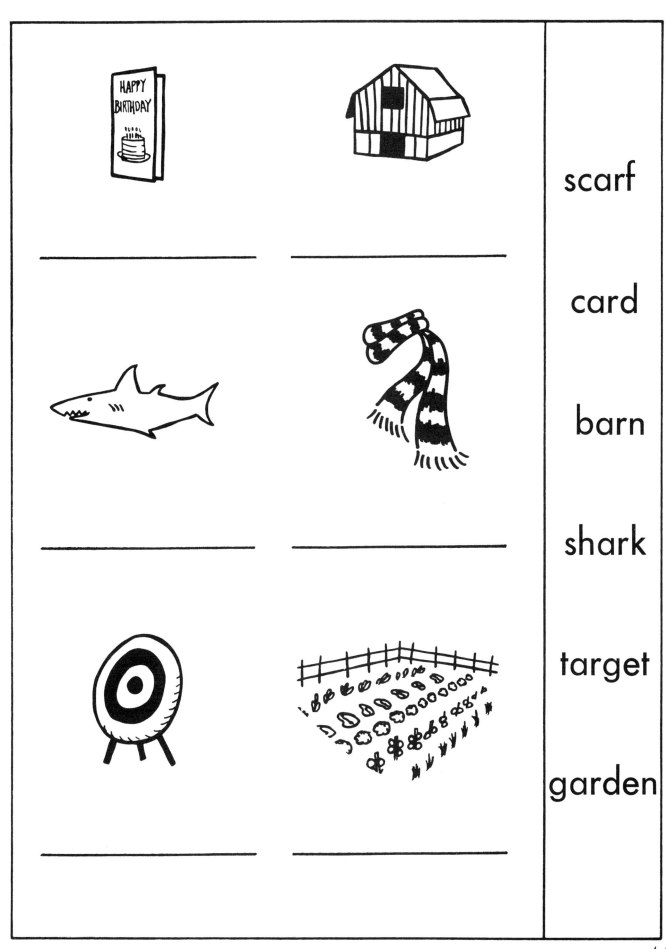

scarf

card

barn

shark

target

garden

is   The
on   scarf
the   cat

dart   The
in   is
the   target

	Yes	No
Is the car on the wheel?	_____	
Is the star on the apple?	_____	
Is the dart on the wheel?	_____	
Is the star on the barn?	_____	
Is the car on the barn?	_____	
Is the dart in the apple?	_____	

The car is blue.
The star is green.
The dart is orange.
The wheel is purple.
The apple is yellow.
The barn is red.

	bath		farm
	barn		fish
	_____		_____

	scarf		white
	shark		witch
	_____		_____

	kettle		teeth
	kitchen		three
	_____		_____

	can		candle
	car		card
	_____		_____

48

corn

horn

cork

fork

torch

porch

horse

thorn

49

_____	_____	_____

The corn is yellow.

The cork is green.

The torch is red.

The fork is orange.

The horse is brown.

The horn is blue.

_____	_____	_____

star   on
The   is
the   cork

is   chick
on   The
horn   the

Now you can read the storybook *The Lost Horse* listed on the back cover.

Three cars are red.
Six cars are blue.

Five stars are green.
Three stars are yellow.

zipper ladder

letter hammer

_____

_____

The ladder is yellow.

The hammer is brown.

The zipper is green.

The letter is blue.

_____

_____

runner   pepper

butter   slipper

grasshopper

_____

_____

_____

_____

55

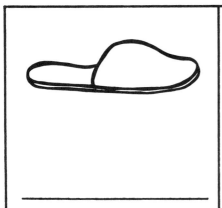

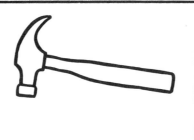

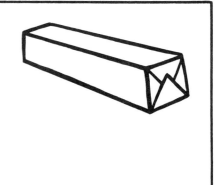

The hammer is brown.

The slipper is red.

The ladder is blue.

The pepper is green.

The zipper is purple.

The butter is yellow.

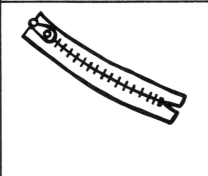

farmer   teacher

reader   sister

_____   _____

_____   _____

winter   hanger

summer   clover

_____   _____

_____   _____

catcher   pitcher

lobster   runner

_____   _____

_____   _____

___

___

___

The runner is blue.

The pepper is green.

The barn is red.

The letter is purple.

The torch is orange.

The porch is yellow.

___

___

___

driver

joker

skater

baker

_____

_____

_____

_____

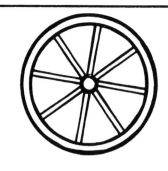

_____ _____ _____

The clover is green.

The target is yellow.

The letter is blue.

The lobster is red.

The whale is black.

The wheel is orange.

_____ _____ _____

Now you can read the storybook _The Brave Hunter_ listed on the back cover.

girl

skirt

bird

shirt

stir

first

third

---

bird

girl

stir

skirt

shirt

third

first

_____

_____

_____

The skirt is orange.

The bird is blue.

The car is red.

The horn is yellow.

The shirt is purple.

The barn is red.

_____

_____

_____

Yes   No

Is the runner on the sandwich? _____

Is the bird on the target? _____

Is the skater on the sandwich? _____

Is the runner on the target? _____

Is the bird on the hanger? _____

Is the skater on the hanger? _____

The hanger is black.
The sandwich is brown.
The target is yellow.
The skater is red.
The runner is green.
The bird is blue.

horse horn ____	ladder lobster ____
splash spaniel ____	pepper pitcher ____
torch thorn ____	shark shirt ____
jar joker ____	cork corn ____

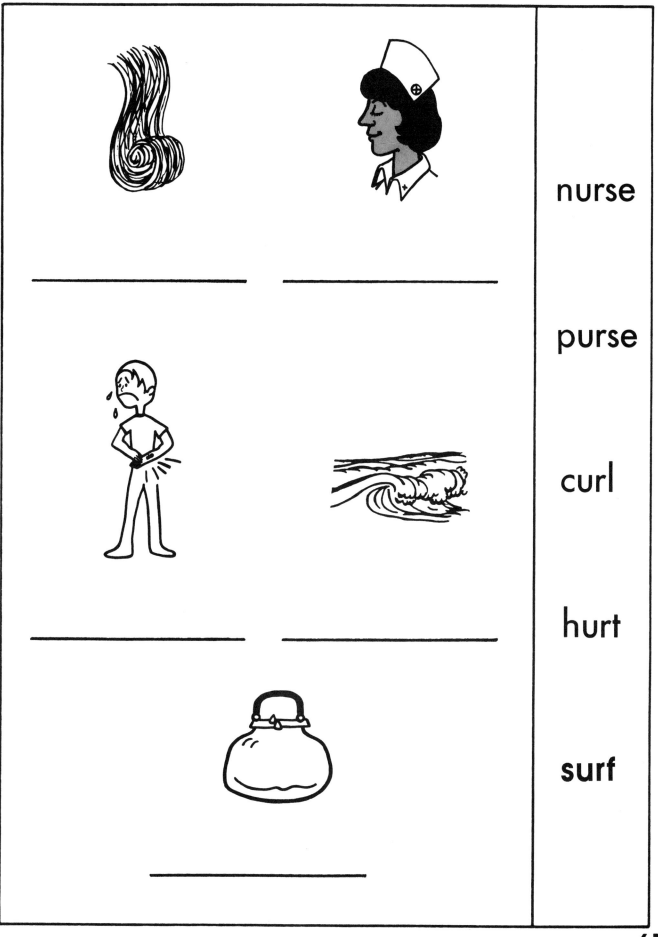

nurse

purse

curl

hurt

surf

_____

_____

_____

The curl is black.

The card is orange.

The jar is green.

The nurse is red.

The girl is yellow.

The purse is brown.

_____

_____

_____

purple   turtle

spur   hamburger

_____   _____

purple

_____   _____

The skirt is purple.

The bird is red.

The fork is yellow.

The turtle is green.

The star is orange.

The surf is blue.

Now you can read the storybook *The Bird Feeder* listed on the back cover.

worm   word

doctor   sailor

tractor

cat

_____

_____

apple   the
The   in
worm   is

The   the
is   **surf**
bird   on

collar   backward

dollar   forward

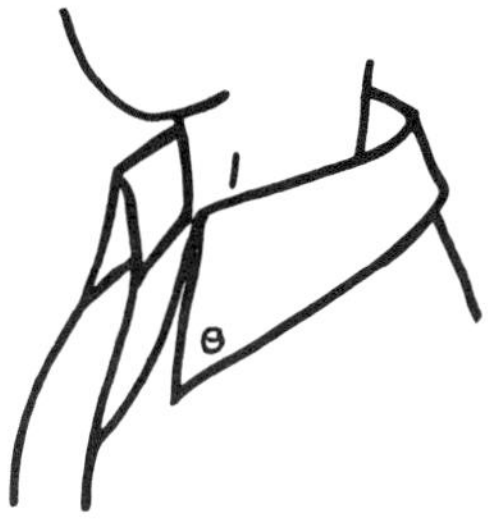

_____   _____

_____   _____

_____   _____   _____

The tractor is orange.

The scarf is blue.

The dollar is green.

The worm is yellow.

The collar is red.

The shark is black.

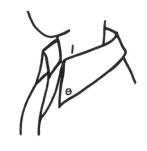

_____   _____   _____

	Yes	No
Is the hamburger on the doctor?	____	
Is the worm on the dollar?	____	
Is the bird on the doctor?	____	
Is the worm on the turtle?	____	
Is the hamburger on the turtle?	____	
Is the bird on the dollar?	____	

The dollar is green.
The bird is red.
The hamburger is brown.
The doctor is blue.
The turtle is yellow.
The worm is orange.

grill

girl

_____

worm

word

_____

horse

hurt

_____

hamburger

hanger

_____

sailor

sailboat

_____

tractor

turtle

_____

clover

collar

_____

forward

farmer

_____

Now you can read the storybook *The Hard Worker* listed on the back cover.

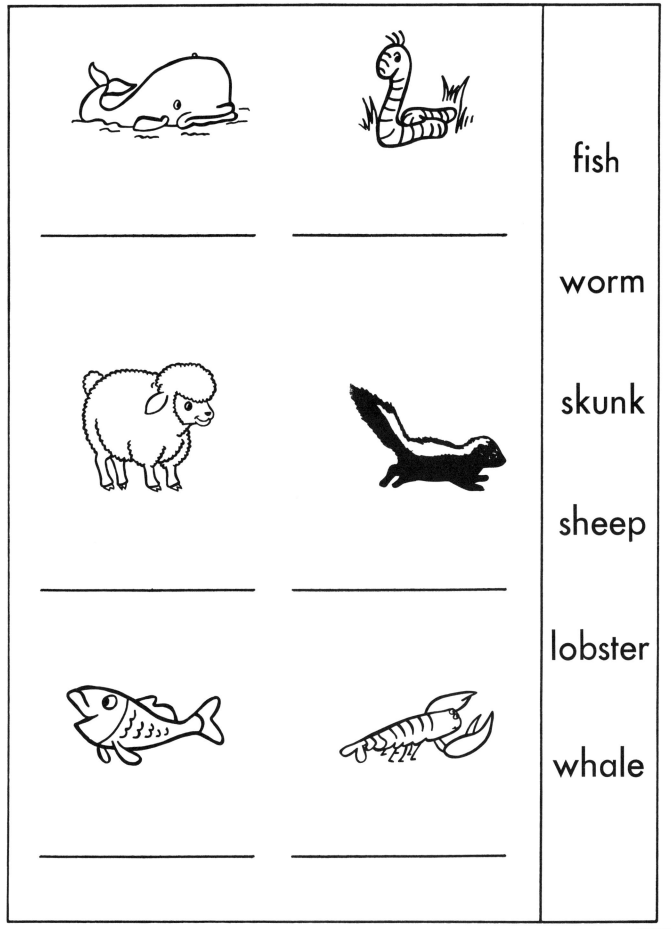

fish

worm

skunk

sheep

lobster

whale

doll dollar		
track tractor		
dock doctor		
sail sailor		

shark

chick

horse

bird

turtle

mink

_____ _____ _____

The car is purple.

The truck is yellow.

The train is red.

The tank is green.

The tractor is orange.

The ship is blue.

_____ _____ _____